take hold!

Also by Lee Bennett Hopkins

Books are by People: Interviews with 104 Authors
and Illustrators of Books for Young Children
More Books by More People: Interviews with
65 Authors of Books for Children

Let Them Be Themselves: Language Arts for
Children in Elementary Schools

Pass the Poetry, Please!

Edited by Lee Bennett Hopkins

Don't You Turn Back:
Poems by Langston Hughes

Girls Can Too! A Book of Poems

Me! A Book of Poems

On Our Way: Poems of Pride and Love

City Talk

take hold!

An Anthology of
Pulitzer Prize
Winning Poems

Selected By

Lee Bennett Hopkins

Thomas Nelson Inc.
Nashville Camden New York

First edition

Library of Congress Cataloging in Publication Data

Hopkins, Lee Bennett, comp.
    Take hold: an anthology of Pulitzer Prize winning poems.

    SUMMARY: Offers selections from the prize-winning works of nineteen American poets.
       1. American poetry—20th century.   2. Pulitzer prizes.   [1. American poetry—Collections]   I. Title.
PS613.H6   811'.5'08   74–10282
ISBN 0–8407–6408–1

ACKNOWLEDGMENTS

Thanks are due to the following for permission to reprint the copyrighted material listed below:

Atheneum Publishers, Inc. for "The Pens," "Tale," "Little Horse," and "Full Moonlight in Spring" from *The Carrier of Ladders* by W. S. Merwin. Copyright © 1967, 1968, 1969, 1970 by W. S. Merwin.

Farrar, Straus & Giroux, Inc. for "Insomnia" and "Letter to N.Y." from *The Complete Poems* by Elizabeth Bishop, copyright © 1940, 1951, 1969 by Elizabeth Bishop, copyright renewed 1968 by Elizabeth Bishop. "The Story Teller," "Spring Thunder," "Afterward," and "Simple Beast" from *Collected Poems* by Mark Van Doren, copyright © 1963 by Mark Van Doren.

Harcourt Brace Jovanovich, Inc. for "Happiness" from *Chicago Poems* by Carl Sandburg, copyright 1916 by Holt, Rinehart and Winston, Inc., copyright 1944 by Carl Sandburg; "Soup" and "Buffalo Dusk" from *Smoke and Steel* by Carl Sandburg, copyright 1920 by Harcourt Brace Jovanovich, Inc., copyright 1948 by Carl Sandburg; "The Dinosaur Bones" and "Webs" from *Good Morning, America*, copyright 1928, 1950 by Carl Sandburg; "Primer Lesson" from *Slabs of the Sunburnt West* by Carl Sandburg, copyright 1922 by Harcourt Brace Jovanovich, Inc., copyright 1950 by Carl Sandburg; "Paper II" from *Complete Poems* by Carl Sandburg, copyright 1950 by Carl Sandburg; "Boy at the Window," copyright 1952 by *The New Yorker Magazine*, Inc. Reprinted from *Things of This World*, © 1956 by Richard Wilbur; "Digging for China" from *Things of This World*, © 1956 by Richard Wilbur.

Harper and Row, Publishers, Inc. for V, IX and X from "The Woman-hood" in *The World of Gwendolyn Brooks* by Gwendolyn Brooks, copyright 1949 by Gwendolyn Brooks.

Holt, Rinehart and Winston, Inc. for "It is Almost the Year Two Thousand," "The Rabbit Hunter," "A Question," and "The Secret Sits" from *The Poetry of Robert Frost*, edited by Edward Connery Lathem. Copyright 1942 by Robert Frost. Copyright © 1969 by Holt, Rinehart and Winston, Inc., copyright © 1970 by Lesley Frost Ballantine.

Houghton Mifflin Company for XII, XV and XVI from "What's O'Clock," by Amy Lowell in *The Complete Poetical Works of Amy Lowell*, copyright 1955 by Harvey H. Bundy and G. d'Andelot Belin, Jr., Trustees of the Estate of Amy Lowell; "Music and Drum," and "Ars Poetica" by Archibald MacLeish from *Collected Poems 1917–1952*. Copyright © 1962 by Archibald MacLeish.

Alfred A. Knopf, Inc., for "Gulls," "Storm's End," "Cantares I and II," and "New Excavations" from *Fiddler's Farewell* by Leonora Speyer. Copyright 1926 by Alfred A. Knopf and renewed 1954 by Leonora Speyer; "XXth Century," and "Moo!" from *Collected Poems* by Robert Hillyer, copyright 1933 and renewed 1961 by Robert Hillyer; "VIII" from "A Sonnet Sequence" from *Collected Verse* by Robert Hillyer, copyright 1933 and renewed 1961 by Robert Hillyer.

Macmillan Publishing Co., Inc. for "The Old Story" by Edwin Arlington Robinson from *Collected Poems* by Edwin Arlington Robinson, coypright 1915 by Edwin Arlington Robinson, renewed 1943 by Ruth Nivison; "Hens in Winter," "The Pheasant," "The Sacrament" by Robert P. Tristram Coffin from *Strange Holiness* by Robert P. Tristram Coffin, copyright 1935 by Macmillan Publishing Co., Inc., renewed 1963 by Margaret Coffin Halvosa.

Norma Millay Ellis for "First Fig," "Second Fig," "Grown Up," and "Portrait by a Neighbor" by Edna St. Vincent Millay from *A Few Figs from Thistles*, Harper and Row, copyright 1922, 1950 by Edna St. Vincent Millay.

New Directions Publishing Corp. for "Calypsos I and II," "The Loving Dexterity," "Exercise No. 2," and "To Flossie" by William Carlos Williams from *Pictures from Brueghel and Other Poems*. Copyright © 1962 by William Carlos Williams.

To Deborah Singer
a
personal
prize

CONTENTS

take hold!

INTRODUCTION

In my many years of work as an educator and writer, I have used poetry with people—poetry written *for* children, poetry written *by* children, poetry written *for* adults, and poetry written *by* adults—and I have come to a conclusion: There is no such thing as poetry written *for*. I've watched five-year-olds become as excited over a poem like Carl Sandburg's "Paper II" as they were about a Mother Goose song. I've seen middle-grade girls and boys enjoy Richard Wright's "Boy at the Window" as much as they have enjoyed the poems appearing in their school textbooks, which were written by "children's poets." I've delighted with junior and senior high-school students as they found, and found themselves in, such poets as Gwendolyn Brooks, William Carlos Williams, and James Wright. I've seen the bright awakening that poetry written "for children" has brought to college students, graduate students, and people whose schooling stopped at the elementary-school level.

Poetry then is not written *for*. Poetry is!

Van Gogh or Warhol, Tchaikovsky or Bacharach did not produce their works for an audience of any specific age, they created from within themselves, and if creative works in music or art by any of our discovered masters, either long past or contemporary, can speak to *people*, so should poetry.

In preparing this collection, I read and reread thousands of poems from volumes that have been awarded the coveted Pulitzer Prize, and from that great body of work I selected those poems that I felt have lasting appeal. Many poems written in the 1920's have as much relevance today as those just being written. Thus, readers can choose from the time and settings they desire, because people themselves are composed of bits and pieces of the past, the present, and even the future.

Within this collection, over fifty years of poetry are represented. The poetry takes all forms, including couplets, haiku, villanelles, sonnets, free verse. It represents American letters at their best and shows that the creation of poetry is as diverse as the creation of people.

In his "Tentative (First Model) Definitions of Poetry," Carl Sandburg states: "Poetry is the report of a nuance between two moments when people say 'Listen!' and 'Did you see it?' 'Did you hear it? What was it?' "

Listen then. Look and see and hear and ask. Grab on. Take hold. Take *your* moments and enjoy them throughout your entire life.

L. B. H.

the 20's

EDWIN ARLINGTON ROBINSON (1869–1935), born in Head Tide, Maine, began writing poetry at the age of eleven. During his second year at Harvard University, when he was twenty-three, his father died, and he left the school to return to Gardiner, Maine, where he had grown up.

In 1896, Robinson went to New York and tried unsuccessfully to earn a living as an inspector in the New York subway. At thirty-five he was rescued from poverty by President Theodore Roosevelt, who gave him a clerkship in the New York Custom House. Four years later he left the job to devote himself to writing.

At the age of fifty-three he won the first of three Pulitzer Prizes for his *Collected Poems* (1922). The two later awards were for *The Man Who Died Twice* (1925) and *Tristram* (1928). Instead of feeling secure, and despite the fact that during the last ten or fifteen years of his life he shared with Robert Frost, another Pulitzer Prize winner, the reputation of being one of America's greatest living poets, he was haunted by his fame. For seven years he drove himself to write an annual volume, but he became more and more of a laconic recluse.

Robinson died in New York City.

The following selections are from Collected Poems.

The House on the Hill

They are all gone away,
    The House is shut and still,
There is nothing more to say.

Through broken walls and gray
    The winds blow bleak and shrill:
They are all gone away.

Nor is there one to-day
    To speak them good or ill:
There is nothing more to say.

Why is it then we stray
    Around the sunken sill?
They are all gone away,

And our poor fancy-play
    For them is wasted skill:
There is nothing more to say.

There is ruin and decay
    In the House on the Hill:
They are all gone away,
There is nothing more to say.

Richard Cory

Whenever Richard Cory went down town,
We people on the pavement looked at him:
He was a gentleman from sole to crown.
Clean favored, and imperially slim.

arrayed

And he was always quietly arrayed,
And he was always human when he talked;
But still he fluttered pulses when he said,
"Good-morning," and he glittered when he walked.

And he was rich—yes, richer than a king—
And admirably schooled in every grace:
In fine, we thought that he was everything
To make us wish that we were in his place.

So on we worked, and waited for the light,
And went without the meat, and cursed the bread,
And Richard Cory, one calm summer night,
Went home and put a bullet through his head.

An Old Story

Strange that I did not know him then,
    That friend of mine!
I did not even show him then
    One friendly sign;

But cursed him for the ways he had
    To make me see
My envy of the praise he had
    For praising me.

I would have rid the earth of him
    Once, in my pride. . . .
I never knew the worth of him
    Until he died.

EDNA ST. VINCENT MILLAY (1892–1950) was born in Rockland, Maine. Encouraged by her mother, she began writing poetry as a child while growing up in Maine and Massachusetts. When she was nineteen, her poem "Renascence," a work of more than two hundred lines about a personal religious experience, brought her immediate acclaim.

Preparatory studies at Barnard introduced her to New York City. In 1917, the year of her graduation from Vassar, her first book of poetry was published. Her fourth volume, *The Harp Weaver,* was awarded the Pulitzer Prize in 1923. The award also included previous works, among which was *A Few Figs from Thistles.*

Besides poetry, Millay wrote opera librettos and radio scripts, and did translations. Her sonnets are said to be in a class with those of Elizabeth Barrett Browning. She died in Austerlitz, New York.

The following selections are from A Few Figs from Thistles.

Grown-Up

Was it for this I uttered prayers,
And sobbed and cursed and kicked the stairs,
That now, domestic as a plate,
I should retire at half-past eight?

First Fig

My candle burns at both ends;
    It will not last the night;
But ah, my foes, and oh, my friends—
    It gives a lovely light!

Second Fig

Safe upon the solid rock the ugly houses stand:
Come and see my shining palace built upon the sand!

Portrait by a Neighbor

Before she has her floor swept
    Or her dishes done,
Any day you'll find her
    A-sunning in the sun!

It's long after midnight
    Her key's in the lock,
And you never see her chimney smoke
    Till past ten o'clock!

She digs in her garden
    With a shovel and a spoon,
She weeds her lazy lettuce
    By the light of the moon,

She walks up the walk
    Like a woman in a dream,
She forgets she borrowed butter
    And pays you back cream!

Her lawn looks like a meadow,
    And if she mows the place
She leaves the clover standing
    And the Queen Anne's lace!

AMY LOWELL (1874–1925) was born in Brookline, Massachusetts. Her family line included famous pioneers, traders, and teachers. A grandfather founded the cotton-manufacturing town of Lowell, Massachusetts. One of her brothers, Abbott Lawrence Lowell, was president of Harvard University. Another, Percival Lowell, was the founder of Lowell Observatory in Flagstaff, Arizona; his mathematical deductions predicted the presence of the planet Pluto, later discovered by an astronomer on the staff of his observatory.

Amy Lowell was educated in private schools and traveled extensively. In 1902, after many years of activity in civic affairs, she discovered that poetry was her "natural mode of expression." In her midthirties, she published her first volume of poetry.

At the beginning of World War I, she went to London, where she became involved in Ezra Pound's "Imagist" movement —an attempt to free poetry of rhyme, regular rhythm, and other traditional limitations. But over the years, the poet could not hold to these beliefs. She tried every poetic device.

She spent the last year of her life writing a two-volume biography of the poet John Keats, a work considered to be one of the greatest biographies in the field of English poetry. Lowell died in 1925. The following year her book of poetry, *What's O'Clock,* was posthumously awarded the Pulitzer Prize.

The following selections are from What's O'Clock.

XIII

Watching the iris,
The faint and fragile petals—
How am I worthy?

XV

Night lies beside me
Chaste and cold as a sharp sword.
It and I alone.

XVI

Last night it rained.
Now, in the desolate dawn,
Crying of blue jays.

Night Clouds

The white mares of the moon rush along the sky
Beating their golden hoofs upon the glass Heavens;
The white mares of the moon are all standing on their
        hind legs
Pawing at the green porcelain doors of the remote Heavens.
Fly, Mares!
Strain your utmost,
Scatter the milky dust of stars,
Or the tiger sun will leap upon you and destroy you
With one lick of his vermilion tongue.

LEONORA SPEYER (1872–1956), born in Washington, D.C., began her career at the age of eighteen as a concert violinist with the Boston Symphony Orchestra. Later she appeared with the New York Philharmonic.

Speyer gave up her music career to write poetry. Her friendship with Amy Lowell sparked her interest and encouraged her to continue writing.

For a period of time the poet taught at Columbia University.

The following selections are from Speyer's 1927 Pulitzer Prize-winning volume, Fiddler's Farewell.

from
Cantares

I

Sweet, my sweet!
Was I fool to show you the sky—
Then strap my wings to your feet?

II

I lied—trusting you knew
I could not lie to you.

Beloved friend, I lied, and am forgiven: but I
Cannot forgive that you believed my lie!

from
Sand-pipings

Gulls

Strong wings in the stormy weather—
Gray stitches that hold
The raveling fabrics of sea and sky
Forever together!

Storm's End

As if engraved upon the dawn,
The sleek gulls stand
Along the rim of an exhausted sea
That rumbles up the sand.

Amazing birds, untired and trim of wing,
Whose round unflinching eyes
Meet like a challenge the leaden-lidded sun
About to rise.

from
Pompeii

New Excavations

A workman with a spade in half a day
Can push two thousand lagging years away.
See, how the tragic villas, one by one,
Like drowsy lizards creep into the sun.

the 30's

ROBERT HILLYER (1895–1961), born in East Orange, New Jersey, was educated at Kent School and Harvard University, where he graduated *cum laude* at the age of twenty-two. That same year his first book was published.

During World War I, Hillyer was an ambulance driver with the American Expeditionary Force in France. He later transferred to the army, where he served as a first lieutenant. After the war he joined the Harvard faculty. By the time he was forty-five years old he had published nineteen books, twelve of which were volumes of poetry.

In 1934 his *Collected Verse* was awarded the Pulitzer Prize.

The following selections are from Collected Verse.

XXth Century

There is no time,
No time,
There is no time,
Not even for a kiss,
Not even for this,
Not even for this rhyme.

It is May
And blossoms sway
In sifted snow
Under the moon.
I only know
That I can not stay,
For today is May
And tomorrow June.

An arrow shot
From an idiot's bow,
That is my lot
And I must go.

There is no time,
No time,
There is no time,
Not even for a kiss,
Not even for this,
Not even for this rhyme,—
     No . . . !

Moo!

Summer is over, the old cow said,
And they'll shut me up in a draughty shed
To milk me by lamplight in the cold,
But I won't give much for I am old.
It's long ago that I came here
Gay and slim as a woodland deer;
It's long ago that I heard the roar
Of Smith's white bull by the sycamore.
And now there are bones where my flesh should be;
My backbone sags like an old roof tree,
And an apple snatched in a moment's frolic
Is just so many days of colic.
I'm neither a Jersey nor Holstein now
But only a faded sort of cow.
My calves are veal and I had as lief
That I could lay me down as beef;
Somehow, they always kill by halves,—
Why not take me when they take my calves?
Birch turns yellow and sumac red,
I've seen this all before, she said,
I'm tired of the field and tired of the shed.
There's no more grass, there's no more clover;
Summer is over, summer is over.

from
A Sonnet Sequence

VIII

Today as I passed through the market-place,
I saw so many things that you might want;
Don't scold me, I was not extravagant,—
A few necessities, that's all, in case
You should be lonely: a papyrus plant
From Egypt; an old saint with a green face;
A unicorn,—quite tame; a bit of lace
Woven from cobwebs; and an elephant.
Please don't be cross; I sold a poem today,
And really you must have these useful things;
Look! here's the best of all; I can not say
Just what it is, but it has lovely wings,
Shines like a rainbow, too. Good God! It's gone.
Kiss me. Don't cry. I'll find another one.

ROBERT P. TRISTRAM COFFIN (1892–1955), a descendant of a Nantucket whaling family, was born in Brunswick, Maine. He was educated at Bowdoin College and Princeton University. In 1921, he became an Oxford University Rhodes Scholar. Besides teaching English he traveled widely, lectured, and gave readings of his work. Many awards and honors were bestowed upon him for his writings, which include, besides poetry, prose, essays, and biographies.

Much of his poetry reflects country life.

The following selections are from the 1936 Pulitzer Prize-winning volume, Strange Holiness.

Hens in Winter

Winter is a far more fit
Time for hens than most admit.
    They are not their best outside,
    The world of trees is much too wide
For their essential comeliness.
One so easily can miss
    Their artificial, tailored graces
    Where a weathered swallow races.
There is in a hen's neat turban
Something planned and very urban.
    Rains and winds and noble weathers
    Rough her temperament and feathers.
And hens depend on company,
Gossip, and garrulity,
    To achieve completest sense
    Of being central and immense

So a henhouse banked with snow
Is the nearest place to go
    To see the virtues of a crowd,
    To hear life have her say aloud.
And nothing's nearer the comic sock
Than a hen that tries to walk
    Through the wild and frigid white
    Blossoms of a Winter night.
The only wild part is the track
She prints on snow in coming back.

The Pheasant

A pheasant cock sprang into view,
A living jewel, up he flew.

His wings laid hold on empty space,
Scorn bulged his eyeballs out with grace.

He was a hymn from tail to beak
With not a tender note or meek.

Then the gun let out its thunder,
The bird descended struck with wonder.

He ran a little, then, amazed,
Settled with his head upraised.

The fierceness flowed out of his eyes
And left them meek and large and wise.

Gentleness relaxed his head,
He lay in jewelled feathers, dead.

The Sacrament

The road was one she saw each day,
But one tall pine tree looked away
Over all the trees like new,
A strange cloud stood up in the blue,
And the sun's light came in under;
The evening might turn one of thunder;
A house nearby had windows burning.

Suddenly beyond the turning
Of the road she saw a sight
Too beautiful to be delight.
A young buck deer with head alert
And eyes so steady that they hurt
Stood and stood and took her in,
Her pulse grew hurried, thin and thin.

Then the creature in a bound
Was gone from sight without a sound;
She knew this instant would remain
A sacrament not touched again.

the 40"s

MARK VAN DOREN (1894-1972) was born in Hope, Illinois. After graduating from the University of Illinois in 1914, he completed his M.A. degree at Columbia University.

During World War I, he served for two years in the infantry, after which he returned to Columbia and was awarded a traveling fellowship. In 1920 he received his Ph.D. from Columbia and taught there until 1959. Among the students he influenced were Jack Kerouac, novelist, and Allen Ginsberg, poet.

In 1940, Van Doren received the Pulitzer Prize for his *Collected Poems*. Besides writing poetry he edited two important collections of writings, *Oxford Book of American Prose* and *Anthology of World Poetry*.

He died in Torrington, Connecticut.

The following selections are from Collected Poems.

The Story-Teller

He talked, and as he talked
Wallpaper came alive;
Suddenly ghosts walked,
And four doors were five;

Calendars ran backward,
And maps had mouths;
Ships went tackward
In a great drowse;

Trains climbed trees,
And soon dripped down
Like honey of bees
On the cold brick town.

He had wakened a worm
In the world's brain,
And nothing stood firm
Until day again.

Spring Thunder

Listen. The wind is still,
And far away in the night—
See! The uplands fill
With a running light.

Open the doors. It is warm;
And where the sky was clear—
Look! The head of a storm
That marches here!

Come under the trembling hedge—
Fast, although you fumble.
There! Did you hear the edge
Of winter crumble?

Simple Beast

With rope, knife, gun, brass knucks, and bloody laws
Earth everywhere is noisy; not with paws
Of leopards silent, not with saber-toothed
Long tigers paced all year upon and smoothed.
That was the age of hunger, when the taken
Fourfoot with a moment's dread was shaken;
Then the slow-closing eyes; then over stones
Time's scattering of the picked, the cleanly bones.
This is the age of anger, when the hail
Beats corn and rose alike, and leaves a trail
More sluttish that it tells man's appetite.
This is the age of gluttony and spite.
With lash and bomb, blue fire and bayonet
Earth everywhere is littered. Earth is wet
With blood not drained for drinking, earth is loud
With sounds not made for hearing, earth is plowed
By steel that will not reap it. Earth is least
Like what earth was when beast was simple beast.

Afterward

The stalls were empty in the shed;
    Nothing grazed beyond the gate.
But there was straw to make a bed,
    And the four bridles dangled straight.

We heard the water running cold,
    As she had left it, round the crocks.
Linen lay for us to fold,
    And there was pepper in the box.

The very trap that he had set
    To catch a mole that loved the lawn
Hung above the passage yet;
    Another mole was boring on.

The wounded deer still fled the dog
    Within the gold and walnut frame;
The Fisherman Among the Fog,
    And The Young Mother, were the same.

We laughed to see a boot behind
    The stove; but then you wept
At your happening to find
    Spectacles where she had slept.

ROBERT FROST (1874–1963) is the only person ever to be awarded four Pulitzer Prizes for his poetry. The prize-winning volumes were *New Hampshire* (1924), *Collected Poems* (1931), *A Further Range* (1937), and *A Witness Tree* (1943).

The poet, born in San Francisco, California, didn't attend school until he was twelve years old and never read a book until he was fourteen.

In 1885, after the death of his father, he moved with his mother and sister to Lawrence, Massachusetts, his father's birthplace. In 1890 his first poem, "La Noche Triste," was published in his high-school paper. In 1892 he graduated from Lawrence High School as covaledictorian. The other student to win this honor was Eleanor White, who became his wife in 1895.

Frost attended Dartmouth College and Harvard University, but left both places before he graduated. He bought a farm in New Hampshire, but in 1912 he moved his family to England. In August of 1914, when war broke out, he returned to the United States, where he learned that Henry Holt and Company was publishing his poetry.

During his lifetime honor upon honor was bestowed upon Frost. On March 26, 1962, on his eighty-eighth birthday, the poet was awarded the Congressional Medal at the White House by President John F. Kennedy.

The following selections are from A Witness Tree.

The Secret Sits

We dance round in a ring and suppose,
But the Secret sits in the middle and knows.

A Question

A voice said, Look me in the stars
And tell me truly, men of earth,
If all the soul-and-body scars
Were not too much to pay for birth.

The Rabbit Hunter

Careless and still
The hunter lurks
With gun depressed,
Facing alone
The alder swamps
Ghastly snow-white.
And his hound works
In the offing there
Like one possessed,
And yelps delight
And sings and romps,
Bringing him on
The shadowy hare
For him to rend
And deal a death
That he nor it
(Nor I) have wit
To comprehend.

It Is Almost the Year Two Thousand

To start the world of old
We had one age of gold
Not labored out of mines,
And some say there are signs
The second such has come,
The true Millennium,
The final golden glow
To end it. And if so
(And science ought to know)
We well may raise our heads
From weeding garden beds
And annotating books
To watch this end de luxe.

the 50's

GWENDOLYN BROOKS (1917–   ), born in Topeka, Kansas, was raised and still lives in Chicago, Illinois. Her first book of poetry, *A Street in Bronzeville,* appeared in 1945. For her second volume, *Annie Allen,* she was awarded the 1950 Pulitzer Prize. This was a significant event in American letters because Brooks was the first black American poet ever to receive this award.

In recent years the poet has been actively involved in teaching and lecturing as well as supporting black self-help efforts via community organizations, writing workshops, and black-owned publishing ventures.

In 1968, Brooks was named Poet Laureate for the State of Illinois, succeeding the late Carl Sandburg. In 1972 her autobiography, *Report from Part One,* appeared. In 1974 the poet was appointed honorary consultant in American letters to the Library of Congress, a position she will hold until 1977.

The following selections are from Annie Allen.

from
The Womanhood

X

Exhaust the little moment. Soon it dies.
And be it gash or gold it will not come
Again in this identical disguise.

from
The Womanhood

V

old laughter

The men and women long ago
In Africa, in Africa,
Knew all there was of joy to know.
In sunny Africa
The spices flew from tree to tree.
The spices trifled in the air
That carelessly
Fondled the twisted hair.

The men and women richly sang
In land of gold and green and red.
The bells of merriment richly rang.

But richness is long dead,
Old laughter chilled, old music done
In bright, bewildered Africa.

The bamboo and the cinnamon
Are sad in Africa.

from

The Womanhood

IX
truth

And if sun comes
How shall we greet him?
Shall we not dread him,
Shall we not fear him
After so lengthy a
Session with shade?

Though we have wept for him,
Though we have prayed
All through the night-years—
What if we wake one shimmering morning to
Hear the fierce hammering
Of his firm knuckles
Hard on the door?

Shall we not shudder?—
Shall we not flee
Into the shelter, the dear thick shelter
Of the familiar
Propitious haze?

Sweet is it, sweet is it
To sleep in the coolness
Of snug unawareness.

The dark hangs heavily
Over the eyes.

CARL SANDBURG (1878–1967) was born in Galesburg, Illinois, a city about 145 miles southwest of Chicago—Abraham Lincoln country—to Swedish immigrant parents.

Leaving school at the age of thirteen, he enlisted in the army during the Spanish-American War. Afterward, he attended college and later wrote for a Chicago newspaper.

Sandburg was virtually unknown in the literary world until a group of his poems appeared in *Poetry* magazine in 1914. The following year his *Collected Poems* was published, leading to a literary career that brought him international fame as a poet, novelist, biographer, historian, journalist, and folk singer.

The author of more than forty books, he twice received the Pulitzer Prize. Once (1940) it was for history, for the last four volumes of his six-volume work, *Abraham Lincoln: The War Years,* a monumental biography that took him thirty years to create. The second time it was for poetry, for *Complete Poems* (1951), a volume of over eight hundred poems written over the forty-year period, 1910–1950.

The poet died at his home in Flat Rock, North Carolina, at the age of eighty-nine. On his death, President Lyndon Baines Johnson issued the statement:

> Carl Sandburg needs no epitaph. It is written for all time in the field, the cities, the face, and heart of the land he loved and the people he celebrated and inspired. With the world we mourn his passing. It is our pride and fortune as Americans that we will always hear Carl Sandburg's voice within ourselves. For he gave us the truest and most enduring vision of our greatness.

Sandburg's birthplace, 331 East Third Street in Galesburg, Illinois, still stands as a monument to the poet. Each year approximately fifteen thousand adults and children visit this memorial to Illinois' Poet Laureate.

The following selections are from Complete Poems.

Happiness

I asked professors who teach the meaning of life to tell me
    what is happiness.
And I went to famous executives who boss the work of
    thousands of men.
They all shook their heads and gave me a smile as though I
    was trying to fool with them.
And then one Sunday afternoon I wandered out along the
    Desplaines river
And I saw a crowd of Hungarians under the trees with their
    women and children and a keg of beer and an accordion.

Soup

I saw a famous man eating soup.
I say he was lifting a fat broth
Into his mouth with a spoon.
His name was in the newspapers that day
Spelled out in tall black headlines
And thousands of people were talking about him.

    When I saw him,
He sat bending his head over a plate
Putting soup in his mouth with a spoon.

Webs

Every man spins a web of light circles
And hangs this web in the sky
Or finds it hanging, already hung for him,
Written as a path for him to travel.
The white spiders know how this geography goes.
Their feet tell them when to spin,
How to weave in a criss-cross
Among elms and maples, among radishes and button weeds,
Among cellar timbers and old shanty doors.
Not only the white spiders, also the yellow and blue,
Also the black and purple spiders
Listen when their feet tell them to spin one.
And while every spider spins a web of light circles
Or finds one already hung for him,
So does every man born under the sky.

The Dinosaur Bones

The dinosaur bones are dusted every day.
The cards tell how old we guess the dinosaur bones are.
Here a head was seven feet long, horns with a hell of a ram,
Humping the humps of the Montana mountains.
                    The respectable school children
Chatter at the heels of their teacher who explains.
The tourists and wonder hunters come with their parasols
And catalogues and arrangements to do the museum
In an hour or two hours.
                    The dinosaur bones
          are dusted
          every day.

Buffalo Dusk

The buffaloes are gone.
And those who saw the buffaloes are gone.
Those who saw the buffaloes by thousands and how they
    pawed the prairie sod into dust with their hoofs, their
    great heads down pawing on in a great pageant of dusk,
Those who saw the buffaloes are gone.
And the buffaloes are gone.

Primer Lesson

Look out how you use proud words.
When you let proud words go, it is
        not easy to call them back.
They wear long boots, hard boots; they
        walk off proud; they can't hear you
        calling—
Look out how you use proud words.

Paper II

I write what I know on one side of the paper
        and what I don't know on the other.
Fire likes dry paper and wet paper laughs at
        fire.
Empty paper sacks say, "Put something in me,
        what are we waiting for?"
Paper sacks packed to the limit say, "We hope
        we don't bust."
Paper people like to meet other paper people.

ARCHIBALD MACLEISH (1892–   ) was born in Glencoe, Illinois. He attended Yale University, after which he entered Harvard Law School. He began a career as an attorney in Boston but gave up law because "he could never believe in the law as a profession." At the age of twenty-five he joined a hospital unit, went to France, and was transferred to the field artillery. By the time World War I ended, he had the rank of captain. Returning to the United States, he taught for one year at Harvard Law School, later working in a variety of government jobs.

From 1944 to 1945 MacLeish was the Assistant Secretary of State and a delegate to the London conference for the drafting of the constitution of UNESCO. From 1949 to 1962 he taught at Amherst College.

MacLeish has won many awards for his multitude of writings. In 1933 he was awarded the Pulitzer Prize for his book-length poem, *Conquistador,* about the Spanish exploration of the New World. The volume stemmed from a 1929 trip in which the poet followed the route of Cortez through Mexico. This was the first of three Pulitzer Prizes he received. The second was awarded in 1953 for his *Collected Poems 1917–1952;* the third for drama (1959) for *J.B.,* a play in verse that was produced on Broadway.

The following selections are from Collected Poems 1917–1952.

Music and Drum

When men turn mob
Drums throb:
When mob turns men
Music again.

When souls become Church
Drums beat the search:
When Church becomes souls
Sweet music tolls.

When State is the master
Drums beat disaster:
When master is man
Music can.

Each to be one,
Each to be whole,
Body and soul,
Music's begun.

Ars Poetica

A poem should be palpable and mute
As a globed fruit,

Dumb
As old medallions to the thumb,

Silent as the sleeve-worn stone
Of casement ledges where the moss has grown—

A poem should be wordless
As the flight of birds.

            *

A poem should be motionless in time
As the moon climbs,

Leaving, as the moon releases
Twig by twig the night-entangled trees,

Leaving, as the moon behind the winter leaves,
Memory by memory the mind—

A poem should be motionless in time
As the moon climbs.

            *

A poem should be equal to:
Not true.

For all the history of grief
An empty doorway and a maple leaf.

For love

The leaning grasses and two lights above the sea—
A poem should not mean
But be.

ELIZABETH BISHOP (1911–   ), born in Worcester, Massachusetts, received a B.A. degree from Vassar College. An extensive world traveler, she lived in Brazil from 1952 to 1967.

Bishop served as poetry consultant to the Library of Congress. Besides poetry she has written short stories which have appeared in *The New Yorker* magazine.

In 1956 she was awarded the Pulitzer Prize for her book *Poems,* a volume that combines two collections, *North and South* and *A Cold Spring.*

The following selections are from Poems.

Insomnia

The moon in the bureau mirror
looks out a million miles
(and perhaps with pride, at herself,
but she never, never smiles)
far and away beyond sleep, or
perhaps she's a daytime sleeper.

By the Universe deserted,
she'd tell it to go to hell,
and she'd find a body of water,
or a mirror, on which to dwell.
So wrap up care in a cobweb
and drop it down the well

into that world inverted
where left is always right,
where the shadows are really the body,
where we stay awake all night,
where the heavens are shallow as the sea
is now deep, and you love me.

Letter to N.Y.

In your next letter I wish you'd say
where you are going and what you are doing;
how are the plays, and after the plays
what other pleasures you're pursuing:

taking cabs in the middle of the night,
driving as if to save your soul
where the road goes round and round the park
and the meter glares like a moral owl,

and the trees look so queer and green
standing alone in big black caves
and suddenly you're in a different place
where everything seems to happen in waves,

and most of the jokes you just can't catch,
like dirty words rubbed off a slate,
and the songs are loud but somehow dim
and it gets so terribly late,

and coming out of the brownstone house
to the gray sidewalk, the watered street,
one side of the buildings rises with the sun
like a glistening field of wheat.

—Wheat, not oats, dear. I'm afraid
if its wheat its none of your sowing,
nevertheless I'd like to know
what you are doing and where you are going.

RICHARD WILBUR (1921–   ) was born in New York City and grew up on a farm in New Jersey. After receiving his B.A. degree from Amherst College in 1942, he served for two years overseas with the United States Armed Forces during World War II. In 1947, after completing an M.A. at Harvard University, he taught at Harvard and Wellesley. Presently he is at Wesleyan University, where he has been a professor of English since 1957.

His first published collection of poems, *The Beautiful Changes, appeared* in 1947, followed by *Ceremony and Other Poems,* and *Walking to Sleep,* a collection of poetry and translations. In 1957 his book of poetry, *Things of This World,* was a triple prize winner. Along with the Pulitzer Prize, the volume received the National Book Award and the Edna St. Vincent Millay Memorial Award.

Besides writing poetry, Wilbur coauthored with Stephen Sondheim the lyrics for the Broadway musical version of *Candide.* He has also written books for children, including *Loudmouse* (1968) and *Opposites* (1973), a book of thirty-nine short poems.

The following selections are from Things of This World.

Boy at the Window

Seeing the snowman standing all alone
In dusk and cold is more than he can bear.
The small boy weeps to hear the wind prepare
A night of gnashings and enormous moan.
His tearful sight can hardly reach to where
The pale-faced figure with bitumen eyes
Returns him such a god-forsaken stare
As outcast Adam gave to Paradise.

The man of snow is, nonetheless, content,
Having no wish to go inside and die.
Still, he is moved to see the youngster cry.
Though frozen water is his element,
He melts enough to drop from one soft eye
A trickle of the purest rain, a tear
For the child at the bright pane surrounded by
Such warmth, such light, such love, and so much fear.

Digging for China

"Far enough down is China," somebody said.
"Dig deep enough and you might see the sky
As clear as the bottom of a well.
Except it would be real—a different sky.
Then you could burrow down until you came
To China! Oh, it's nothing like New Jersey.
There's people, trees, and houses, and all that,
But much, much different. Nothing looks the same."

I went and got the trowel out of the shed
And sweated like a coolie all that morning,
Digging a hole beside the lilac-bush,
Down on my hands and knees. It was a sort
Of praying, I suspect. I watched my hand
Dig deep and darker, and I tried and tried
To dream a place where nothing was the same.
The trowel never did break through to blue.

Before the dream could weary of itself
My eyes were tired of looking into darkness,
My sunbaked head of hanging down a hole.
I stood up in a place I had forgotten,
Blinking and staggering while the earth went round
And showed me silver barns, the fields dozing
In palls of brightness, patens growing and gone
In the tides of leaves, and the whole sky china blue.
Until I got my balance back again
All that I saw was China, China, China.

the 60's

PHYLLIS MCGINLEY (1905–   ), born in Ontario, Oregon, is known for her many forms of writing. Besides poetry she has written over a dozen children's books, essays, lyrics for a Broadway revue, and many stories that have appeared in such magazines as *Good Housekeeping, The New Yorker, McCalls,* and *Vogue.*

She always wanted to become a poet and was rhyming words at the age of six. While in college she began selling poetry to various national magazines. Encouraged by her success, she came to New York in 1928 and taught high school in New Rochelle. McGinley then moved to New York City to work in advertising, later becoming the poetry editor of *Town and Country* magazine.

In 1961 the poet was awarded the Pulitzer Prize for *Times Three: Selected Verse from Three Decades: 1930–1950,* in which, as in most of her work, McGinley wittily describes the virtues of our American way of life.

The following selections are from Times Three.

from
New England Pilgrimage

The Customs of the Country

Connecticut, with much at stake,
prefers to call a pool a lake,
But in New Hampshire and beyond
They like to call a lake a pond.

from
Speaking of Television

Almost Any
Evening

On all the channels,
Nothing but panels!

from
Speaking of Television

Reflections Dental

How pure, how beautiful, how fine
Do teeth on television shine!
No flutist flutes, no dancer twirls,
But comes equipped with matching pearls.
Gleeful announcers all are born
With sets like rows of hybrid corn.
Clowns, critics, clergy, commentators,
Ventriloquists and roller skaters,
M.C.s who beat their palms together,
The girl who diagrams the weather,
The crooner crooning for his supper—
All flash white treasures, lower and upper.
With miles of smiles the airwaves teem,
And each an orthodontist's dream.

'Twould please my eye as gold a miser's—
One charmer with uncapped incisors.

WILLIAM CARLOS WILLIAMS (1883–1963), a New Jersey physician, wrote in many forms—poetry, autobiography, plays, essays, short stories, the novel, and personal interpretations of history.

Born in Rutherford, New Jersey, he received his preparatory schooling in Geneva, Switzerland. He held an M.D. degree from the University of Pennsylvania and did graduate work in pediatrics at the University of Leipzig, in Germany.

Like his lifelong friend, Ezra Pound, Williams constantly sought a purely American idiom for poetry. He had an enormous influence on young poets, who often sent him poems and received back from him long, warm letters.

In 1963, two months after his death, he was posthumously awarded the Pulitzer Prize for *Pictures from Brueghel: Collected Poems 1950–1962.* This volume of free verse, with its characteristic sharp, short lines, brings together the poetry that he wrote during the last decade of his life.

The following selections are from Pictures from Brueghel.

Calypsos

II

Love the sun
come
up in

the morning
and
in

the evening
zippy zappy
it goes

Calypsos

III

We watched
a red rooster
with

two hens
back
of the museum

at
St. Croix
flap his

wings
zippy zappy
and crow

The Loving
Dexterity

The flower
    fallen
she saw it

    where
it lay
    a pink petal

intact
    deftly
placed it

    on
its stem
    again

Exercise No. 2

The metal smokestack
of my neighbor's chimney
greets me among the new leaves

it is a small house
adjacent to my bigger one
I have come in 3 years

to know much of her
an old lady as I am an old man
we greet each other

across the hedge
my wife gives her flowers
we have never visited each other

To Flossie

who showed me
    a bunch of garden roses
she was keeping
    on ice

against an appointment
    with friends
for supper
    day after tomorrow

aren't they beautiful
    you can't
smell them
    because they're so cold

but aren't they
    in wax
paper for the
    moment beautiful

LOUIS SIMPSON (1923–   ), born in Jamaica, West Indies, began writing poetry at the age of thirteen. His varied life experiences include work in journalism, in the export-import business, and in book publishing. During World War II he was a rifleman in the United States Army and twice received the Purple Heart.

After attending Columbia University, where he received both his M.A. and his doctoral degree, he began teaching at the University of California at Berkeley.

His fourth collection of poetry, *At the End of the Open Road,* received the Pulitzer Prize in 1964. About poetry, Simpson states: "Most poetry is mere fantasy; most prose is merely reporting the surface of things. We are still waiting for the poetry of feeling, words as common as a loaf of bread, which yet give off vibrations."

The poet is also the author of the novel *Riverside Drive* (1962).

The following selections are from At the End of the Open Road.

American Poetry

Whatever it is, it must have
A stomach that can digest
Rubber, coal, uranium, moons, poems.

Like the shark, it contains a shoe.
It must swim for miles through the desert
Uttering cries that are almost human.

In the Suburbs

There's no way out.
You were born to waste your life.
You were born to this middleclass life

As others before you
Were born to walk in procession
To the temple, singing.

Frogs

The storm broke, and it rained,
And water rose in the pool,
And frogs hopped into the gutter,

With their skins of yellow and green,
And just their eyes shining above the surface
Of the warm solution of slime.

At night, when fireflies trace
Light-lines between the trees and flowers
Exhaling perfume,

The frogs speak to each other
In rhythm. The sound is monstrous,
But their voices are filled with satisfaction.

In the city I pine for the country;
In the country I long for conversation—
Our happy croaking.

The Redwoods

Mountains are moving, rivers
are hurrying. But we
are still.

We have the thoughts of giants—
clouds, and at night the stars.

And we have names—guttural, grotesque—
Hamet, Og—names with no syllables.

And perish, one by one, our roots
gnawed by the mice. And fall.

And are too slow for death, and change
to stone. Or else too quick,

like candles in a fire. Giants
are lonely. We have waited long

for someone. By our waiting, surely
there must be someone at whose touch

our boughs would bend; and hands
to gather us; a spirit

to whom we are light as the hawthorn tree.
O if there is a poet

let him come now! We stand at the Pacific
like great unmarried girls,

turning in our heads the stars and clouds,
considering whom to please.

RICHARD EBERHART (1904–   ) was born in Austin, Minnesota. In addition to writing poetry and plays, he has worked as a floorwalker, as a deck boy on tramp steamers, has been private tutor to the son of King Prajadhipok of Siam, served as lieutenant commander in the United States Navy, and has taught at various schools and universities in America.

The following selections are from his 1966 Pulitzer Prize-winning volume, Selected Poems.

Forms of the Human

I wanted to be more human
For I felt I thought too much
And for all the thinking I did—
More rabbits in the same hutch.

And how to be more human, I said?
I will tell you the way, I said.
I know how to do it, I said.
But what I said was not what I did.

I took an old garden hoe
And dug the earth, and planted there,
Not forgetting the compost too,
Three small beans that one might grow.

Three grew tall, but one was wild
So I cut off the other two,
And now I have a wild bean flower
The sweetest that ever grew.

On a Squirrel Crossing the Road
in Autumn, in New England

It is what he does not know,
Crossing the road under the elm trees,
About the mechanism of my car,
About the Commonwealth of Massachusetts,
About Mozart, India, Arcturus,

That wins my praise. I engage
At once in a whirling squirrel-praise.

He obeys the orders of nature
Without knowing them.
It is what he does not know
That makes him beautiful.
Such a knot of little purposeful nature!

I who can see him as he cannot see himself
Repose in the ignorance that is his blessing.

It is what man does not know of God
Composes the visible poem of the world.

        . . . Just missed him!

Hark Back

To have stepped lightly among European marbles
Dwelling in a pantheon of air;

To have altered the gods in a fact of being;

To have envisaged the marriage
Of everything new with the old,

And sprung a free spirit in the world

Is to have caught my own spirit
On a bicycle in the morning

Riding out of Paris,
Heading South.

My flesh felt so good
I was my own god.

from
Attitudes

New England Protestant

When Aunt Emily died, her husband would not look at her.
Uncle Peter, inarticulate in his cold intelligence,
Conceded few flowers, arranged the simplest service.
Only the intimate members of the family came.

Then the small procession went to the family grave.
No word was spoken but the parson's solemn few.
Silence, order, a prim dryness, not a tear.
We left the old man standing alone there.

the **70's**

W. S. MERWIN (1927–   ) was born in New York City and grew up in Union City, New Jersey, and Scranton, Pennsylvania.

From 1949 to 1951, he worked as a tutor in France, Portugal, and Majorca. After this period he devoted himself to translating and to writing articles, prose, radio scripts for the British Broadcasting Corporation, and, of course, poetry.

His first book of poetry, *The Mask of Janus,* appeared in 1952. At that time, W. H. Auden, the Pulitzer Prize-winning poet, hailed Merwin as a new "mythological" poet who spoke in universal and impersonal terms.

In 1971 he was awarded the Pulitzer Prize for his sixth book of poetry, *The Carrier of Ladders.*

The following selections are from The Carrier of Ladders.

The Pens

In the city of fire the eyes
look upward
there is no memory
except the smoke writing writing *wait*
wai
w
under the light that has
the stars inside it
the white
invisible stars they also
writing

and unable to read

Tale

After many winters the moss
finds the sawdust crushed bark chips
and says old friend
old friend

Full Moonlight in Spring

Night sends this white eye
to her brother the king of the snow

Little Horse

You come from some other forest
do you
little horse
think how long I have known these
deep dead leaves
without meeting you

I belong to no one
I would have wished for you if I had known how
what a long time the place was empty
even in my sleep
and loving it as I did
I could not have told what was missing

what can I show you
I will not ask you if you will stay
or if you will come again
I will not try to hold you
I hope you will come with me to where I stand
often sleeping and waking
by the patient water
that has no father nor mother

JAMES WRIGHT (1927–   ), born in Martins Ferry, Ohio, was educated at Kenyon College. He also attended the University of Vienna as a Fulbright Fellow and the University of Washington.

In addition to serving in the United States Army, he has traveled extensively and has taught at both the University of Minnesota and New York's Hunter College.

Wright's first book of poetry, *The Green Wall*, appeared in 1957, followed by *St. Judas* (1959), *The Branch Will Not Break* (1963), and *Shall We Gather at the River* (1968). The poems from all these works, plus thirty-three of the author's new poems, are included in his 1972 Pulitzer Prize-winning volume, *Collected Poems*.

The following selections are from Collected Poems.

March

A bear under the snow
Turns over to yawn.
It's been a long, hard rest.

Once, as she lay asleep, her cubs fell
Out of her hair,
And she did not know them.

It is hard to breathe
In a tight grave:

So she roars,
And the roof breaks.
Dark rivers and leaves
Pour down.

When the wind opens its doors
In its own good time,
The cubs follow that relaxed and beautiful woman
Outside to the unfamiliar cities
Of moss.

Spring Images

Two athletes
Are dancing in the cathedral
Of the wind.

A butterfly lights on the branch
Of your green voice.

Small antelopes
Fall asleep in the ashes
Of the moon.

Depressed by a Book of Bad Poetry, I Walk Toward an Unused Pasture and Invite the Insects to Join Me

Relieved, I let the book fall behind a stone.
I climb a slight rise of grass.
I do not want to distrub the ants
Who are walking single file up the fence post,
Carrying small white petals,
Casting shadows so frail that I can see through them.
I close my eyes for a moment, and listen.
The old grasshoppers
Are tired, they leap heavily now,
Their thighs are burdened.
I want to hear them, they have clear sounds to make.
Then lovely, far off, a dark cricket begins
In the maple trees.

To a Fugitive

The night you got away, I dreamed you rose
Out of the earth to lean on a young tree.
Then they were there, hulking the moon away,
The great dogs rooting, snuffing up the grass.
You raise a hand, hungry to hold your lips
Out of the wailing air; but lights begin
Spidering the ground; oh they come closing in,
The beam searches your face like fingertips.

Hurry, Maguire, hammer the body down,
Crouch to the wall again, shackle the cold
Machine guns and the sheriff and the cars:
Divide the bright bars of the cornered bone,
Strip, run for it, break the last law, unfold,
Dart down the alley, race between the stars.

ABOUT THE PULITZER PRIZE

The Pulitzer Prizes, annual awards given in the United States to honor distinguished achievements in journalism, literature, drama, and music, were established by Joseph Pulitzer [1] (1847–1911), a Hungarian-born immigrant who became famous as a newspaper publisher. He founded the *St. Louis Post-Dispatch* and the former *New York World*.

Pulitzer's will provided $2 million for Columbia University to establish a school of journalism, and specified that after the school had operated for at least three years, prizes should be awarded for the advancement of America's achievements.

The Columbia School of Journalism was founded in 1912. The first Pulitzer Prize was awarded in 1917. Since then the Pulitzer Prizes have been given annually on the first Monday in May on the recommendation of Columbia University's Advisory Board on the Pulitzer Prizes. The recommendations are judged by a group of editors for the journalism awards, and a group of writers, critics, and/or professionals for the others. Judges may decide not to give an award in one or more categories if they feel there has been no worthy entry during the current year.

The Pulitzer Prize for Poetry was established in 1922, but earlier awards were made through gifts of the Poetry Society. The awards made in 1918 and 1919 are carried in the Pulitzer Prize records.

The following is a complete listing of the Pulitzer Prizes for Poetry. An asterisk preceding a poet's name indicates that poems from that particular work are contained in this volume.

1918   Sara Teasdale, *Love Songs.*

1919   Margaret Widdemer, *Old Road to Paradise.*
        Carl Sandburg, *Corn Huskers.*

1920   No award.

[1] Pronounced PULL-it-sir.

1921   No award.

1922   * Edwin Arlington Robinson, *Collected Poems.*

1923   * Edna St. Vincent Millay, *The Ballad of the Harp Weaver; A Few Figs from Thistles;* eight sonnets in *American Poetry; A Miscellany.*

1924   Robert Frost, *New Hampshire.*

1925   Edwin Arlington Robinson, *The Man Who Died Twice.*

1926   * Amy Lowell, *What's O'Clock.*

1927   * Leonora Speyer, *Fiddler's Farewell.*

1928   Edwin Arlington Robinson, *Tristram.*

1929   Stephen Vincent Benet, *John Brown's Body.*

1930   Conrad Aiken, *Selected Poems.*

1931   Robert Frost, *Collected Poems.*

1932   George Dillon, *The Flowering Stone.*

1933   Archibald MacLeish, *Conquistador.*

1934   * Robert Hillyer, *Collected Verse.*

1935   Audrey Wurdemann, *Bright Ambush.*

1936   * Robert P. Tristram Coffin, *Strange Holiness.*

1937   Robert Frost, *A Further Range.*

1938   Marya Zaturenska, *Cold Morning Sky.*

1939   John Gould Fletcher, *Selected Poems.*

1940   * Mark Van Doren, *Collected Poems.*

1941   Leonard Bacon, *Sunderland Capture.*

1942   William Rose Benét, *The Dust Which Is God.*

1943   * Robert Frost, *A Witness Tree.*

1944   Stephen Vincent Benét, *Western Star.*

1945   Karl Shapiro, *V-Letter and Other Poems.*

1946   No award.

1947   Robert Lowell, *Lord Weary's Castle.*

1948	W. H. Auden, *The Age of Anxiety.*
1949	Peter Viereck, *Terror and Decorum.*
1950	* Gwendolyn Brooks, *Annie Allen.*
1951	* Carl Sandburg, *Complete Poems.*
1952	Marianne Moore, *Collected Poems.*
1953	* Archibald MacLeish, *Collected Poems 1917–1952.*
1954	Theodore Roethke, *The Waking: Poems 1933–1953.*
1955	Wallace Stevens, *Collected Poems.*
1956	* Elizabeth Bishop, *Poems: North and South* and *A Cold Spring*
1957	* Richard Wilbur, *Things of This World.*
1958	Robert Penn Warren, *Promises: Poems 1954–1956.*
1959	Stanley Kunitz, *Selected Poems, 1928–1958.*
1960	William DeWitt Snodgrass, *Heart's Needle.*
1961	* Phyllis McGinley, *Times Three: Selected Verse from Three Decades.*
1962	Alan Dugan, *Poems.*
1963	* William Carlos Williams, *Pictures from Brueghel.*
1964	* Louis Simpson, *At the End of the Open Road.*
1965	John Berryman, *Seventy-Seven Dream Songs.*
1966	* Richard Eberhart, *Selected Poems (1930–1965).*
1967	Anne Sexton, *Live or Die.*
1968	Anthony Hecht, *The Hard Hours.*
1969	George Oppen, *Of Being Numerous.*
1970	Richard Howard, *Untitled Subjects.*
1971	* W. S. Merwin, *The Carrier of Ladders.*
1972	* James Wright, *Collected Poems.*
1973	Maxine Kumin, *Up Country: Poems of New England.*
1974	Robert Lowell, *The Dolphin.*

INDEX OF POETS

INDEX OF TITLES

INDEX OF FIRST LINES